JONAH'S OCEAN FRIENDS

5 Bedtime Stories from the Deep

BLUME POTTER

INTRODUCTION

Are you searching for a bedtime book that not only delights your children or grandchildren but also instills timeless values from the Bible? Jonah's Ocean Friends: 5 Bedtime Stories from the Deep is the perfect choice. This beautifully crafted collection retells the beloved story of Jonah and the great fish through the eyes of various sea creatures, offering a unique and engaging perspective on important themes such as obedience, repentance, forgiveness, and second chances.

Each chapter is designed to capture young imaginations while gently guiding them toward understanding the deeper messages of faith and God's love. The stories are filled with adventure, warmth, and a touch of whimsy, making them ideal for children aged 3 to 8. As you read these tales together, you'll not only be sharing precious moments but also planting seeds of spiritual wisdom that will grow as your little ones do.

Make bedtime a time of peace, learning, and connection with God's word. Let Jonah's Ocean Friends be the book your children and grandchildren look forward to each night, nurturing both their hearts and minds in the most delightful way.

CHAPTER ONE:
THE WHALE'S TALE

In the deep blue ocean, where the sunlight barely reached, lived a mighty whale. He was the largest creature in the sea, with a heart as big as a mountain and a gentle nature that made him a friend to all the fish. The whale loved swimming through the vast waters, feeling the currents tickle his fins, and listening to the songs of the ocean.

But one day, something unusual happened. As the whale was gliding peacefully through the waves, he felt a strange tug in his heart. It was as if something, or someone, was calling to him. The whale didn't know what it meant, but he felt an urge to follow this call, even though it made him feel uneasy.

As he swam further, he noticed a small ship being tossed around by a fierce storm. The whale watched as the sailors frantically tried to keep the ship afloat. Suddenly, a man was thrown overboard, plunging into the dark, stormy waters. The whale could see the man struggling, but something inside told him this was no ordinary man—this was someone special.

Without thinking, the whale opened his enormous mouth and swallowed the man whole. At first, the whale was confused. Why had he done such a thing? He had never swallowed anything other than tiny fish and krill. But deep down, he felt that this was something he was meant to do, though he didn't fully understand why.

Inside the whale's belly, the man—Jonah—began to pray. He was scared and alone, but he knew that God had a plan for him. The whale could feel the man's fear, but he could also sense Jonah's growing trust in something greater.

As the days passed, the whale started to realize that he was part of something much bigger than himself. He wasn't just a creature of the sea; he was a part of God's plan. Jonah needed time to think and pray, and the whale was giving him that time.

Three days later, the strange tug in the whale's heart returned, but this time it was different. It was a gentle nudge, guiding him toward the shore. The whale obeyed, swimming toward the shallow waters. When he reached the beach, he felt the same nudge, telling him it was time to release Jonah.

With a mighty push, the whale opened his mouth, and Jonah was safely deposited on the sandy shore. The whale watched as Jonah stood up and looked around, grateful and determined. The whale didn't need to understand everything; he just knew he had done what he was supposed to do.

As the whale swam back into the deep blue ocean, he felt a sense of peace. He might never fully understand his role, but he knew it was important. Obedience, he realized, wasn't just about following orders—it was about being part of something bigger, something filled with purpose and meaning.

And so, the whale continued his journey through the ocean, knowing that sometimes, the most important things we do are the ones we don't fully understand.

CHAPTER TWO:
THE CURIOUS DOLPHINS

In the sparkling waters of the ocean, not far from where the great whale carried Jonah in his belly, a pod of dolphins swam playfully through the waves. They were known for their joyful spirits and curious nature, always eager to explore and understand the world around them.

One day, as they darted through the sea, the dolphins noticed the massive whale moving slowly and deliberately through the water. This wasn't the usual carefree swimming they were used to seeing from their giant friend. The dolphins were intrigued. They swam closer, eager to discover what was going on.

As they approached the whale, they heard a faint sound—a soft murmur that seemed to come from deep within the whale. It wasn't the usual rumblings of the sea; it was something different, something that felt almost... human. The dolphins, puzzled and intrigued, began to swim alongside the whale, listening closely.

"What could it be?" one dolphin asked, flipping in the water.

"It sounds like a voice," another replied. "But how can there be a voice inside a whale?"

The dolphins were full of questions. They circled the whale, trying to make sense of what they were hearing.

As they swam closer, they realized that the voice was not just any voice—it was a prayer. A prayer filled with sorrow, hope, and a deep sense of longing.

The dolphins, with their gentle hearts, could sense the emotions behind the prayer. They felt the sadness of someone who had made a mistake, the hope of someone seeking a second chance, and the strength of a spirit trying to make things right.

"What do you think it means?" one dolphin asked, tilting its head.

"I think," another dolphin said thoughtfully, "that it's about asking for forgiveness. The one inside the whale must have done something wrong and is now trying to make it right."

The dolphins continued to swim alongside the whale, their curiosity turning into a deeper understanding. They began to discuss the ideas of repentance and forgiveness, concepts that were new to them.

"Is it possible for someone to be forgiven, even after making a big mistake?" one dolphin wondered.

"Perhaps," another dolphin replied, "that's what this journey is about. Maybe the one inside the whale is learning that no matter how big the mistake, there is always a chance to make things right if you truly seek forgiveness."

The dolphins, with their joyful spirits, felt a sense of peace wash over them as they swam. They realized that forgiveness was a powerful thing, something that could bring light to even the darkest places.

As they continued to accompany the whale on its journey, the dolphins felt grateful for the lesson they were learning. They understood now that everyone makes mistakes, but what matters most is the willingness to turn around, seek forgiveness, and try to do better.

And so, the dolphins swam on, their hearts light and their spirits high, knowing that they were part of something important—something that was helping not just the one inside the whale, but also themselves, to grow and understand the true meaning of repentance and forgiveness.

CHAPTER THREE:
THE PROTECTIVE OCTOPUS

Deep beneath the ocean's surface, where the light barely reached, lived a wise and watchful octopus. With its eight long arms and keen eyes, the octopus was known for its ability to sense danger and protect its underwater friends. The octopus spent its days gliding quietly through the water, always alert and ready to help those in need.

One day, as the octopus was exploring the ocean floor, it noticed the great whale swimming by. The whale moved slowly, and there was something different about its journey. Curious, the octopus swam closer and soon realized that the whale was carrying something precious inside—a man named Jonah.

The octopus could sense the importance of Jonah's presence within the whale. It understood that Jonah's journey was a special one, guided by a power far greater than any in the sea. The octopus knew it had a role to play in this divine plan.

As the whale continued its journey, other sea creatures began to draw near, curious about the strange sounds coming from inside the whale. Some fish darted closer, while others circled around, trying to figure out what was happening. The octopus realized it had to act quickly to keep the whale and Jonah safe.

With its long arms, the octopus gently but firmly waved the curious creatures away. It created a protective barrier around the whale, ensuring that nothing would disturb

Jonah's time of reflection and prayer. The octopus moved gracefully through the water, always keeping a close watch on the whale's surroundings.

The other sea creatures, seeing the octopus's protective stance, respected its authority and kept their distance. They knew that the octopus was wise and that its actions were for the greater good. Slowly, the waters around the whale grew calm and peaceful, with the octopus standing guard.

As the days passed, the octopus never left the whale's side. It knew that even though Jonah was inside a dark and unfamiliar place, he was under God's protection. The octopus understood that sometimes, God's care comes in ways we don't expect—like being kept safe inside a whale in the middle of the ocean.

Through its actions, the octopus taught a valuable lesson: that God's protection is always with us, even in the most unlikely places. Whether in the depths of the sea or the challenges we face in life, God is always watching over us, guiding us, and keeping us safe.

When the time came for Jonah to leave the whale and continue his journey, the octopus felt a deep sense of peace. It had fulfilled its role in God's plan, and now it could return to its quiet life in the ocean, knowing that it had been part of something truly special.

And so, the protective octopus swam away, its heart full of gratitude for the opportunity to serve and protect. It knew that God's care is always present, no matter where we are, and that we are never truly alone.

CHAPTER FOUR:
THE GUIDING STARFISH

In the vast ocean, where the currents flowed gently and the waves whispered secrets of the deep, lived a wise old starfish. The starfish had seen many things during its long life, from the bustling coral reefs to the calm, sandy shores. It moved slowly, but its mind was sharp, and it knew that every creature, no matter how small, had a purpose in the grand design of life.

One day, as the starfish rested on a rock near the ocean floor, it noticed a great whale passing by. The whale was carrying something important—a man named Jonah. The starfish sensed that Jonah's journey was nearing its end and that the whale needed to find the right place to release him.

The starfish knew that the shores of Nineveh were where Jonah was meant to go. It also knew that the whale, though mighty and strong, might need a little guidance to find the way. So, the starfish decided to help, knowing that even its small actions could make a big difference.

As the whale swam, the starfish gently detached itself from the rock and began to drift with the current, moving closer to the whale. The starfish knew that its place was to be a guide, to show the way when the path seemed unclear.

The whale, sensing the starfish's presence, slowed its pace. The starfish positioned itself in front of the whale, using the gentle currents to guide the massive creature toward the shores of Nineveh. The whale followed, trusting in the starfish's wisdom.

As they traveled together, the starfish reflected on how God had given it this important task. It knew that sometimes, the smallest creatures were given the most important roles. The starfish felt honored to be part of this plan, guiding Jonah to the place where he could continue his journey and fulfill his purpose.

When they finally reached the shores of Nineveh, the starfish felt a sense of peace. It had completed its task, and the whale was now ready to release Jonah. The starfish watched as the whale gently opened its mouth, allowing Jonah to step out onto the sandy shore.

The starfish knew that its role, though small, was vital in helping Jonah reach his destination. It understood that every creature, no matter how big or small, has a role to play in God's plan. The starfish taught the whale—and Jonah—a valuable lesson about guidance and the importance of following God's directions, no matter how small or large the task.

With its job done, the starfish slowly drifted back into the depths of the ocean, content in knowing that it had helped fulfill a greater purpose. It returned to its quiet life on the ocean floor, where it would continue to be a guide for those who needed it, always ready to play its part in the grand design of life.

CHAPTER FIVE:
THE SECOND CHANCE

The sun was beginning to rise, casting a golden glow over the calm waters as the great whale approached the shores of Nineveh. Inside the whale, Jonah knew that his journey was about to take a new turn. He had spent three days in the belly of the whale, reflecting on his choices and praying for forgiveness. Now, it was time to start again.

The whale, guided by the wise starfish, had brought Jonah to the exact spot where he needed to be. As the whale neared the shore, it gently opened its mouth, and Jonah stepped out onto the soft, sandy beach. The sea creatures, who had been watching and helping throughout the journey, gathered around the shoreline, curious to see what would happen next.

Jonah stood still for a moment, feeling the warmth of the sun on his face and the solid ground beneath his feet. He knew that he had been given a second chance—a chance to make things right and to follow God's call. He turned to look at the sea, where the whale and his ocean friends watched him with understanding eyes.

With a grateful heart, Jonah began to walk towards the city of Nineveh, knowing that his mission was far from over. The sea creatures watched as Jonah disappeared from view, feeling a sense of pride and peace. They had all played a part in Jonah's journey, helping him when he needed it most.

As the whale slowly turned back towards the deep ocean, it reflected on the meaning of second chances. It understood that everyone makes mistakes, but it's never too late to turn back, seek forgiveness, and start anew. Jonah had been given a second chance, and so had the people of Nineveh, who would soon hear his message.

The sea creatures, each in their own way, had learned about the importance of forgiveness and the power of obeying God's call. They knew that their actions, no matter how small, had made a difference in Jonah's life and in the lives of many others.

As the ocean returned to its gentle rhythm, the whale, the starfish, the dolphins, and the octopus all went back to their lives in the sea, knowing that they had been part of something much bigger than themselves. They had helped Jonah find his way, and in doing so, they had learned valuable lessons about God's love, mercy, and the gift of a second chance.

And so, the story of Jonah and his ocean friends came to an end, but the lessons they learned would stay with them forever—a reminder that with God, there is always a chance to start again, to be forgiven, and to fulfill the purpose we are given.